Lightning Bolt

How Tanks Work

Walt Brody

Lerner Publications ◆ Minneapolis

Lerner Publications Company
A division of Lerner Publishing Group, Inc.
241 First Avenue North
Minneapolis, MN 55401 USA

For reading levels and more information, look up this title at www.lernerbooks.com.

Library of Congress Cataloging-in-Publication Data

Names: Brody, Walt, 1978- author.
Title: How tanks work / Walt Brody.
Description: Minneapolis, MN : Lerner Publications, [2020] | Series: Lightning bolt books. Military machines | Includes bibliographical references and index.
Identifiers: LCCN 2018035866 (print) | LCCN 2018039824 (ebook) | ISBN 9781541556560 (eb pdf) | ISBN 9781541555662 (lb : alk. paper)
Subjects: LCSH: Tanks (Military science)—History—Juvenile literature.
Classification: LCC UG446.5 (ebook) | LCC UG446.5 .B6844 2020 (print) | DDC 623.74/752—dc23

LC record available at https://lccn.loc.gov/2018035866

Manufactured in the United States of America
1-46021-43344-10/25/2018

Table of Contents

The Mighty Tank

Tanks can drive over almost anything. They move on metal loops called tracks. Tall hills, deep sand, or big rocks are no problem for tanks. Tanks can even roll over cars!

Tanks are military vehicles. Soldiers around the world use tanks. **The tanks protect the soldiers.**

Most tanks have huge guns called cannons. Cannons shoot shells. The shells can destroy other tanks.

A cannon is a gun that is too heavy for a person to carry.

A gunner loads a shell into the cannon. Shells are large bullets that explode.

A tank's crew has a commander, a driver, and a gunner. The driver drives the tank. The gunner controls the cannon. The commander tells the rest of the crew what to do.

A History of Tanks

Inventor Leonardo da Vinci had an idea in 1485. He drew an armored tank with guns, but he didn't build it.

Britain and France built the first tanks. The two countries made more than sixty-five hundred tanks for World War I (1914-1918).

Tanks keep soldiers safe during battles.

In World War II (1939–1945), large groups of tanks battled other tanks. The largest tank battle in World War II had about six thousand tanks.

Modern tanks weigh less than tanks did in World War II. They can move much faster. Tanks can go 45 miles (72 km) an hour on flat ground.

Tanks can move fast on spinning tracks.

Parts of a Tank

Tanks are covered in armor. The armor is made of layers of steel and other strong materials.

A soldier makes sure a tank's engine is ready to go.

A mighty engine powers a tank. The engine is in the back of the vehicle. Tank engines have 1,500 horsepower.

Tracks are made of metal so they won't easily break.

Tracks help tanks drive where cars can't go. A tank's tracks are wide. They help the tank grip the ground. Wide tracks also keep a heavy tank from sinking into soft ground.

A tank's cannon is on a turret.
The turret turns to aim the cannon. The cannon can hit a target more than 2.5 miles (4 km) away.
Some turrets can turn in a complete circle.

Tanks in Action

During wars, tanks fight against other tanks. They can attack buildings and other vehicles too.

There are about sixty thousand active tanks in the world. The United States has almost three thousand tanks. China has about seventy-five hundred tanks. That's more tanks than any other country has.

A group of tanks is a tough fighting force!

Tanks can't go everywhere. They can't climb steep mountains or plow through thick jungles. Tanks work best on flat, open land.

Tanks of the future might be drones. Drone tanks could fight battles while their crews stay safe. Drone tanks are mighty military machines!

Soldiers can control this drone tank from far away.

Tank Diagram

Tank Facts

- In 1903, H. G. Wells wrote "The Land Ironclads." The story was about an armored war machine that drove on land. An ironclad was an armored military boat.
- Tanks use high-tech gear to attack enemies. Computers help the gunner aim and shoot. Modern tanks miss their targets less often than World War II tanks did.
- Some tanks carry temporary bridges. The tank can place the bridge across a river in less than two minutes. Then other vehicles can cross the river.

Glossary

armor: the strong outer layer of a tank

cannon: a large gun attached to wheels or a vehicle

commander: the leader of a tank's crew

crew: a group of people who control a tank

drone: a vehicle that people control from far away

horsepower: a unit that measures the power of an engine. The term *horsepower* comes from comparing the power of an engine to the power of one horse.

turret: the top part of a tank that the cannon is attached to

vehicle: something to move people or things

Further Reading

Bambo Jambo: Tank for Kids
http://bambo-jambo.com/military-equipment/tank-for-kids/

History for Kids: World War II Tanks
http://www.historyforkids.net/world-war-2-tanks.html

Kiddle: Main Battle Tank Facts
https://kids.kiddle.co/Main_battle_tank

Morey, Allan. *Tanks*. Minneapolis: Bullfrog Books, 2015.

Silverman, Buffy. *How Do Tanks Work?* Minneapolis: Lerner Publications, 2016.

Slingerland, Janet. *Military Vehicles*. Chicago: Norwood House, 2018.

Index

Photo Acknowledgments

Image credits: U.S. Army/Pfc Austin Anyzeski, 11th ACR, p. 2; U.S. Marine Corps/Cpl. Dallas Johnson, p. 4; U.S. Marine Corps/Lance Cpl. Angel Travis, p. 5; Stocktrek Images/Getty Images, p. 6; U.S. Army/Amanda Kim Stairrett, p. 7; DEA Picture Library/Getty Images, p. 8; Hulton Archive/Stringer/Getty Images, p. 9; Sovfoto/Universal Images Group/Getty Images, p. 10; U.S. Army/Sgt. Leon Cook, p. 11; Artur Widak/NurPhoto/Getty Images, p. 12; U.S. Army/Sgt. 1st Class Jon Soucy, p. 13; U.S. Marine Corps/Cpl. Alexander Sturdivant, p. 14; U.S. Marine Corps/Lance Cpl. Julio McGraw, p. 15; Joe Raedle/Getty Images, p. 16; Anton Novoderezhkin/TASS/Getty Images, p. 17; U.S. Marine Corps/Lance Cpl. Kathryn Howard, p. 18; Christophe Morin/IP3/Getty Images, p. 19; U.S. Army/Pfc. Daniel Parrott, p. 20; U.S. Army/Eugen Warkentin, p. 22.

Cover: Tramino/Getty Images.

Main body text set in Billy Infant regular 28/36. Typeface provided by SparkType.